DEIDRE SCHERER

WORK IN FABRIC & THREAD

C&T PUBLISHING

Editor: Annie Nelson
Technical Editor: Sally Loss Lanzarotti
Book Design: Riba Taylor © 1997 C&T Publishing
Cover Production: John M. Cram
Photography by Jeff Baird unless otherwise noted.

Front cover image: **SWEET AIR** 1997, fabric and thread, 8" x 7"
Collection of Beth Larson and John Lueders
Back cover image: **UNSAID** 1997, fabric and thread, 11" x 10"
Collection of Mary Curzan
(In galleries and museums the vertical
measurement precedes the horizontal.)

Quotation on page 28 from *Matisse on Art,* Revised Edition by Jack Flam.
Copyright © 1995 by Jack Flam. Reprinted with permission
of George Borchardt Agency.
Quotations on pages 50 and 51 from *Songs of Experience* by Priscilla
McCutcheon and Margaret Fowler. Copyright © 1990 by Ballantine Books,
Inc. Reprinted with permission of Ballantine Books, a Division of Random
House Inc.

Library of Congress Cataloging-in-Publication Data
Scherer, Deidre, 1944-
      Deidre Scherer: work in fabric & thread / Deidre Scherer.
            p.   cm.
      Includes index and bibliographical references.
      ISBN   1-57120-044-4
      1. Scherer. Deidre,   1944-   —Themes,
      motives.   2. Aged in art.
      3. Fabric pictures—United States.   I. Title.
      NK9315.S34 1998
      746.3' 92—dc21   97-40165
                                          CIP

Mylar is a registered trademark of E.I. duPont de Nemours & Company.
Pfaff is a registered trademark of Pfaff Corporation.

Published by C&T Publishing, Inc.
P.O. Box 1456
Lafayette, CA 94549

Printed in HongKong
10   9   8   7   6   5   4   3   2   1

DEIDRE SCHERER

WORK IN FABRIC & THREAD

RECOLLECTION 1997, fabric and thread, 11" x 10"
Artist's collection

Acknowledgments

I gratefully acknowledge the practical and spiritual support from my friends and family: Steve Levine, Barbara Fisher, Sarenna Stein, Karen Thalin, Meg Storey, Alison Freeland, Lucy Fradkin, Arthur Simms, Patricia and Prentice Claflin, Deborah Kruger, Lenore O'Connell, Susan Osgood, Sheila Ross, Nancy Burgess, Sally Warren, Carol Sevick, Sheila Hutchins, Rebecca Graves, Annie Gibson, Corina Willette, Gianna Dorman, Janice Scherer, Pam Mayer, and Annie Nelson and the C&T family.

I give thanks for my mentors, my models, and teachers: Sandy Ware and Linden Lodge, Alice Forrett, Jess Farmer, Mary Fillion, Gertrude Ploof, Elizabeth Layton, Joseph Goto, Carol Emory, Susan McClean, Esther Burstein, Alice Holway, Lillian Thayer, Elizabeth Spencer, Marianna Heaney, Miriam Harris, Sonia Cullinen, Gertrude Wolfe, Constance Pace, Charlotte and Richard Thalin, Marguerite Dowell, Faye and Dr. Steve Geller, Stanley and Theodora Feldberg, Dr. Paul Rhodes, Dr. Ira Byock, James Poulos, Sigmund Abeles, Mr. C., Kim Banister, Hildegard Bachert, Claudia Karabaic Sargent, Lanny Lasky, Anna Land, and Cicely Aikman and Fred Scherer.

In memory of my Nana,
Constance Gillis Sampiere,
and all grandmothers and wise women.

Contents

Preface

Like a hand-held retrospective, this book presents key images that chronicle my twenty year passion with the medium of fabric and thread. This collection traces the gradual progression of my technique and of finding my voice.

As the aging face has become my most significant subject matter, it gives me particular joy to make the elders and the mentors more visible and accessible. Images of aging have the power to influence social change by aesthetically and psychologically challenging ageism.

Repeatedly I am drawn to the detailed and pointilistic patterning of printed cloth. Fabric has become the perfect vehicle with which to translate elements that are complex, non-verbal, and even invisible. Visually compelling images can provide the impetus for that unique and personal journey through art. These images pull me forward in my life as I pull them forward through fabric and thread.

Drawing

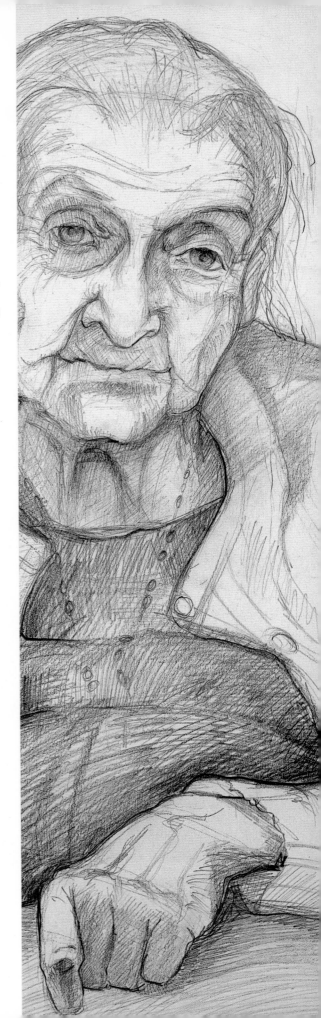

GREAT GRANDFATHER GILLIS 1960, pastel on paper, 23" x 17"
Artist's collection

10

I have always drawn. I was drawing before I learned to speak. I was three years old before I spoke, and in my early school years I remember needing remedial speech therapy. I drew on the back of my Uncle Vincent's photography paper. Some of these drawings I still have—they're full of visual music.

In kindergarten, the school principal hung my first solo exhibition on the walls of her office. Already, I was being singled out as the class artist. By age sixteen I was bartering with my orthodontist: an oil painting in exchange for several payments on my braces. During high school, I found refuge within a close-knit art department. "Remember, there is much strength in talented hands," read the message Mr. Caivano signed in my yearbook.

Throughout my childhood, my father worked at the Museum of Natural History in New York City. He painted dioramas, worked on exhibit preparation, and restored museum artifacts. When I played hooky, I had access to the whole museum. I would passionately sketch the art, clothing, and artifacts of many ancient cultures. I studied a world of mediums, including sand painting, beadwork, quill work, bark painting, wood and ivory carvings, clay, and textiles. At home I roamed the woods, made trails, built miniature villages or life-sized dwellings, and got into stream beds and played with the clay. I have always worked with a visual language. Drawing was the key to all the mediums, and the core of all of my activities.

Many of my works begin with a drawing. Draw-ings are the blueprints for my work. In essence, each of my images are "drawn" three times: first in pencil, chalk, or craypa, then with scis-sors, and finally with my sewing machine. The first drawing is done directly from the model. It takes at least two hours to make a drawing with enough information to translate into fabric. This requires that I describe, through graphite, how the light is hitting, and how the form and structure is occurring.

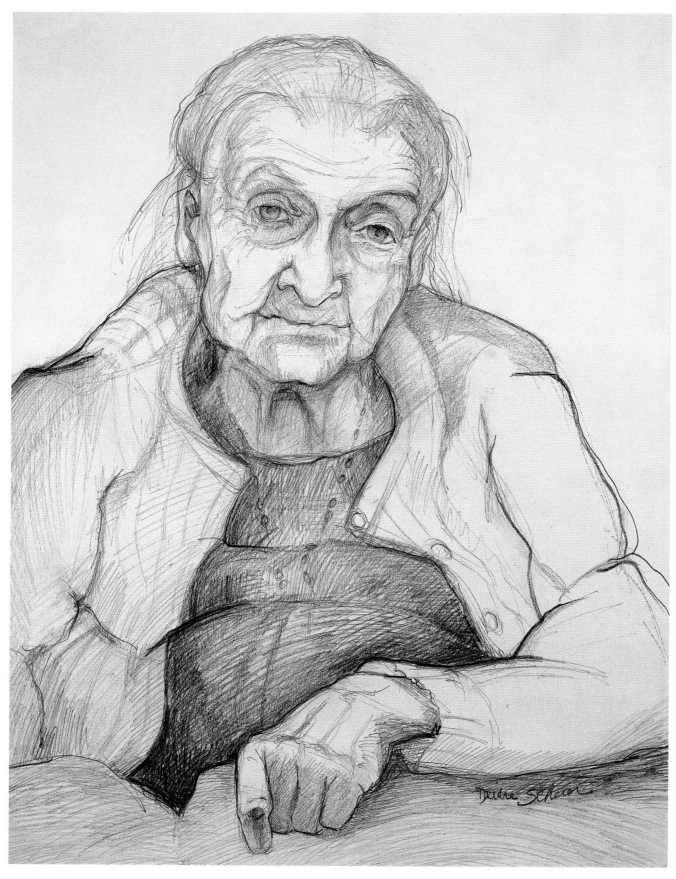

MARY DEGUIRE 1982, graphite on paper, 21½" x 16"
Artist's collection

MARY D. 1982
Fabric and thread, 36½" x 26"
Collection of Dr.'s Grace
and Warren Wilner

If my model and I don't have the time and space to share, I work from a photograph. Photographs are a window into someone's spirit, and I have learned how to read and use them. However, unlike a photograph, a drawing unfolds in a unique way. It is a layering process that slowly occurs over two or three hours. Stories are exchanged, and even the silence is rich with meaning. If time is available to do more than one drawing, I often leave one with the model.

SAGE 1988
Fabric and thread, 26" x 20"
Collection of George W. Crockett

DRAWING OF MARY Y. 1983
Graphite on paper, 22" x 19"
Artist's collection

I treasure my drawings, because I can work from them repeatedly, moving them through different translations, or reawakening the moment I first witnessed. The same drawing of Mary Deguire was used for the first fabric version of her in 1982, called *Mary D.*, and again in 1988 for *Sage*. *Mary Y.* appears in her first translation in 1984 and reappears in 1987 in *Map of the Year 100*.

MAP OF THE YEAR 100 (Detail) 1987
Fabric and thread, 33" x 31"
Collection of James J. McGovern

MARY Y. 1984
Fabric and thread, 10" x 10"
Private collection

DRAWING OF ALICE 1988, graphite on paper, 20" x 16"
Artist's collection

Every time I sit down to draw, I push beyond the fear that I can't do it. When looking at a blank page, I walk past the voices that say, "This isn't possible—I'm not capable." With each stroke of my pencil or crayon, I hang onto sharing the moment with that person. When drawing, I subvert my insecurities with my desire and responsibility to really know that moment, that person's essence and soul. Capturing that specific person's likeness is secondary to finding their universal quality.

People inevitably move from their starting pose and may never get back to that first position. Recapturing a model's pose is difficult, because I'll have to continue to draw them from memory long after they've moved. In the process, I get to see more than the original contours, more than one profile. It's almost a sculptural sensation, because I am able to see around the forms that I am drawing.

While drawing a model's nose, she may reach up and rub her nose. Then I will work underneath her chin, and she might brush away something on her chin. Although she cannot see my drawing, she is reacting to where I had been focused, as if my pencil had literally touched her face. It is a psychic connection between us.

The importance of drawing is what I want to stress. I remind myself that I am drawing for me, for my life, and for my work. I am not drawing to flatter a model, to please a teacher, a parent, or anyone else. They are notations. They are working drawings, and the end product is secondary.

LEGACY (first version)
1989, fabric and thread,
27" x 22", no longer exists

LEGACY 1990
Fabric and thread
25½" x 21"
Private collection

WATERCOLOR OF CICELY 1992, watercolor on paper, 10" x 7"
Artist's collection

Because my drawings are primarily done in black and white, they allow for many interpretations, moods, and emotions to spring from the same drawing. Although black and white provides the most mobility, I do use craypas or watercolor to suggest the color memory of a place or specific moment. *Line of Thought*, with its high color, is most obviously based on *Watercolor of Cicely*. The hot orange of her scarf and the golden reflection in the shadow of her face remind me of a late fall afternoon, or the glow of candlelight.

LINE OF THOUGHT 1992, fabric and thread, 9½" x 8"
Private collection

I love to visit museums, access their print and drawing departments, or look at books to absorb how other artists draw. As a young artist, I studied firsthand the unframed drawings of Van Gogh and Cezanne at the Art Institute of Chicago. Needing heroes to emulate, I absorbed the work and words of women artists. Through the years, I have collected books on the letters, memoirs, and life-works of Paula Modersohn-Becker, Kaethe Kollwitz, Suzanne Valadon,·Georgia O' Keeffe, Alice Neel, and Faith Ringgold. It is important to distinguish when we are under the influence of another artist and give credit to their work as in an homage or pastiche.

NUDE 1993, craypa on paper, 17" x 14"
Artist's collection

Sometimes I join drawing groups that share the expense of a model. In one such instance, a dozen artists, who met regularly, were each required to bring a log for the wood stove. From that session came the *Nude* drawing, which inspired *Sunflower Curtain*.

By practicing my drawing skills, by drawing for myself and finding the joy of drawing, I have come to know that my own level of satisfaction and confidence is all that counts. There is nothing to live up to except my own needs. This experience of freedom carries over into the act of cutting fabric.

SUNFLOWER CURTAIN 1993, fabric and thread, 20" x 18"
Private collection

I do not use a pencil to first draw on the fabric, and then follow a line with my scissors. Nor do I use templates or project my drawing onto the fabric with a projector. Instead, I draw directly into the fabric with my scissors. People have asked me, "How did you get that pattern?" thinking that I have cut one out of paper, pinned it to the fabric, and then cut around it. That would completely kill the thrill of cutting spontaneously into the freshly ironed surface of the fabric.

With scissors, I create contours out of a flat field of color, whether solid, or full of texture and pattern. In each color field, I establish a line in three dimensions. I cut the fabric while holding it aloft, so that I can rotate it freely as I cut.

DRAWING OF JESS 1985, graphite on paper, 28" x 23"
Artist's collection

As I intently study the drawing or photograph of the model, I determine what area to describe with what particular field of color. My eye chooses interior contours; it is a moment of truth. If I get it wrong, I've learned to throw it on the floor, start over, and cut again. If I happen to end up with a rough color transition, I pull out more fabric, find the right color, and patch it from behind or add a layer over it. I hardly ever rip out; it's too tedious.

READING 1993, fabric and thread, 25" x 20"
Collection of Elizabeth W. Hopkins

I draw directly again with my sewing machine, placing the graphite drawing within my full view just behind the machine. While covering the raw edge of the fabric with a zigzag stitch for structural reasons, I also modulate the visual transition between one color field and another. I can either shade and soften, or highlight and sharpen, depending on the color of thread I'm using and the length and width of the stitch. By continually graduating and changing the settings on my machine, a contour can be emphasized by the thickness of the stitch or blended by a more open and lighter application.

Using a sewing machine to draw is extraordinary. With almost every other drawing tool you are, in effect, pushing or pulling the tool. With a pencil, chisel, or brush, you are pushing or pulling, and leaving a mark right along the same line of your action, whereas with the sewing machine, the mark is happening between my fingers as a result of a complex manipulation.

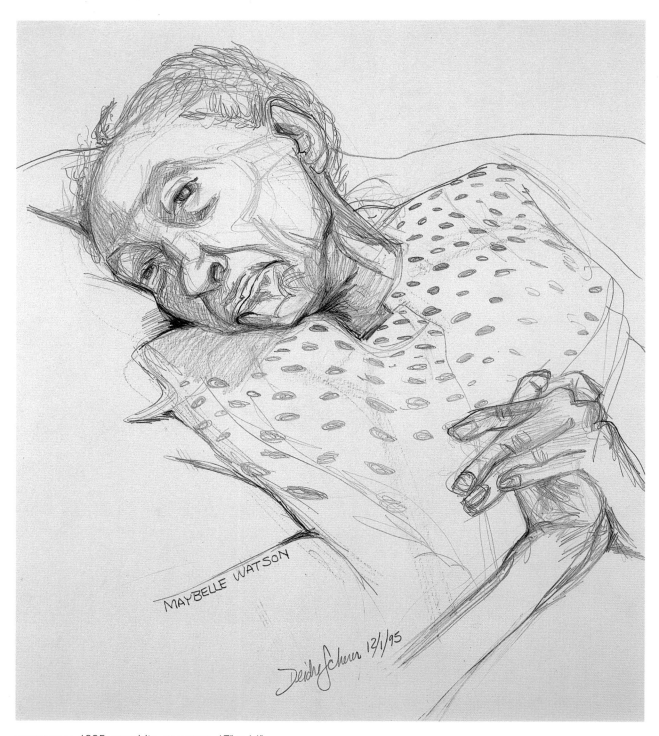

MAYBELLE 1995, graphite on paper, 17" x 14"
Artist's collection

In the winter of 1995, my husband Steve and I were introduced to the Hanover Infirmary by gerontologist Dr. Paul Rhodes. The Hanover Infirmary is located in a poor, rural village in Lucea, Jamaica in the West Indies. To start, I gathered information by drawing for five days.

This was my first visual research within a new world, and a very different world than that of Vermont or the States. In the process of sitting, witnessing, and drawing, I opened to the spirituality of the elder residents at the Hanover Infirmary.

HANOVER HANDS 1996, fabric and thread, 27" x 30"
Artist's collection

Upon returning home, I translated two of the drawings into fabric. Maybelle was ninety-three when I drew her, and just completely remarkable in her presence. She was not able to get off her bed, but could bolt straight up from her waist and engage me about my drawing. She had never seen herself in a photo or a mirror.

HANOVER HANDS
(Detail, first version) 1996
Fabric and thread, 23" x 20"
No longer exists

Kenuth was blind. I always share a drawing with my models, periodically holding it up and saying, "Here's how far I've gotten" or "How do you think this looks?" Since I knew I couldn't do that with him, I gave him my pencils—he turned them and touched them. I gave him my kneaded eraser, my sharpener, and the paper I was using because it had a tooth to it. Then he sat.

KENUTH JOHNSON 1995
Graphite on paper, 17" x 14"
Artist's collection

MORNING IN DECEMBER 1996, fabric and thread, 15" x 13"
Artist's collection

There was nothing else I could give to Kenuth, and every stroke with my pencil felt like this incredible responsibility. While I was drawing him, this awareness grew. Was I getting his ear right? Did I have the shape of his skull? Was I establishing the way that he holds his head? How do I draw blind eyes? The other side of this situation is that Kenuth was in the Hanover Infirmary because he has cataracts. In the States, a cataract operation is an outpatient procedure. Maybe in some way my work will bring attention to his needs and to the needs of this poor, yet extraordinary, community.

The character of a face *in a drawing depends not upon its various proportions but upon a spiritual light that it reflects. So much so, that two drawings of the same face may represent the same character though drawn in different proportions. No leaf of a fig tree is identical to any other, each has a form of its own, but each one cries out: Fig tree.*

HENRI MATISSE

Early Work

SELF-PORTRAIT 1965, graphite on paper, 29" x 24"
Artist's collection

Although I have been making art all my life, to consciously claim that "I am an artist!" proves to be difficult. I equate being an artist with being a creator, and being a creator is as close to God as you can get. Craftsperson, artisan, quilter, and even fiber artist all sound safer. Yet staying humble and never using the artist word blocks me from recognizing my responsibility as an artist. By recognizing myself as an artist, I am finally free and accountable to do my work. By visualizing and naming my place in life, I take myself and my art seriously, which in turn requires that others will.

I had a formal education with an emphasis on drawing at the Rhode Island School of Design. In the ceramic studio, and the printmaking, illustration, and painting departments, I reveled in diverse mediums (but interestingly, not in textiles). In fact my only experience with the textile department occurred when friends set up a loom for me on which I made myself a long, multicolored scarf.

During my first pregnancy, I picked up batik. While working with this new medium, my hand and eye were freed from the well-ingrained approaches to drawing developed through my academic education. Being right handed, I found that drawing with flowing hot wax was similar to drawing with my left hand or my foot.

Because of mild dyslexia and a particular lack of patience, I had no confidence with sewing machines. I had been a home economics dropout back in middle school. During the sewing class segments, when asked to sew a hem on a skirt, I was the only one who came up with a laundry bag with a zipper! It felt like a breakthrough to finally learn the delicate control of a sewing machine.

Eventually I found my way to fabric in an unexpected manner. When my oldest daughter, Gianna, turned three, I observed her looking at fabric books. This variety of baby's first books were, quite frankly, unimaginative and ugly. I decided to make a book for her which became the origin of *The Beast at Bed's End*.

Each fabric panel measures eleven by thirteen inches. The first panel shows a patchwork character, Patches, springing forth from a crazy quilt; she is magically animated by the moonlight and emerges in the same way that clouds take form and become figures in the sky. As Patches moves across her patchwork landscape, she comes upon a black cat that has also evolved from the background of the crazy quilt. Patches and the Cat continue along their fabric path, discovering the Bird, and then the Horse. Together all four friends come upon the Dragon, who is also awakened from the quilt pieces. Their journey occurs at night, which is the time of limitlessness, fantasy, and dream.

In the final panels, they approach a hillside and greet the rising sun. At first they're delighted by the brilliant sun, but soon realize that it forces them to scatter and dissolve back into the quilt shapes from which they'd come.

This work is perhaps the most courageous I have ever done. Although it was a beginning, I did not let my unfamiliarity or my clumsiness stop me. Now I look back at those six years of development and see a primitive but beautiful work. *The Beast at Bed's End* is an analogy of how I pull things out of fabric. *The Beast at Bed's End* must receive credit as the beginning of my entire romance with fabric. In this work, I honed my skills and began to glimpse how incredibly flexible and plastic this medium could be. My roots are in painting, and now my paint is fabric. I don't use the term appliqué, because so many people get sidetracked by a certain stereotypical image associated with that term.

For a while *The Beast at Bed's End* stayed in book form; I had sewn every page together in the manner of a folded accordion. Eventually, a museum calling for art quilts inspired me to back and tack the pieces together. It is the only quilt I've ever made. To me it is still a storyboard that reads across without words, in comic book fashion. Later, poet and mime artist Peter Gould translated my images to words and wrote a twenty-four stanza poem, "The Beast at Bed's End."

Throughout the evolution of this piece, I had two more daughters and two failed marriages. At one point, although physically exhausted, I drove across the country looking for "community." I searched for an environment that would be healthy and supportive of my children. Instinctively, I sought allies for making art—I was drawn to the hills of Vermont. With Vermont's relatively long winters and rural character, I found an isolation that cultivated creativity.

I am capable of working through difficult times. During these times, I built several important pieces. In practice, my work in fiber serves as a rudder. While going through life crises, I may not be able to do much else, yet I've done the work. Being a single parent, however trying, gave me an extended childhood. There is a certain shelter in the mother/child enclosure. Gianna, Corina, and Sarenna were my first audience and gave credence to my inner world and dreams. It was also at this time that I established my habit of working at night.

(Opposite)
THE BEAST AT BED'S END
1972–1978, fabric and thread, 76" x 67"
Collection of Robert and JoAnn Smith

THE BEAST AT BED'S END

MOON PLACE 1978, fabric and thread, 26" x 33½"
Private collection

As I gained fluency in fabric, I worked on a series of birds—"stretched my wings." The glimpses in my mind's eye of what could be said in fabric encouraged me to keep stretching beyond the known path.

Fabric is a warm and absorbent visual medium: it pulls one's eye to its surface and it awakens tactile memories. From birth onward, we have all been wrapped in material. Our skin has an intimate relationship with fabric. Even without literally touching it, we "feel" fabric, and our bodies participate in knowing what we are perceiving optically. This increases the depth of possible responses that people bring to fiberwork—it gets under the skin.

My fascination with fabric grew. I searched for subjects and issues that would engage me on both intellectual and emotional levels—I played with landscape. *West River* began with a quick drawing of the river while taking a trip up Route 30 from Brattleboro, Vermont. Being unsatisfied with its short depth of field, I eventually removed it from the frame and reworked the foreground. By adding highlights to the trees, and drawing more heavily with my machine, I added definition which raised the foreground as well as the energy of the piece. *West River #2* captures the movement and power of that body of water rushing between the hills.

WEST RIVER 1978
Fabric and thread
27" x 30½"
No longer exists

WEST RIVER #2 1981, fabric and thread, 27" x 30½"
Collection of Steve Levine

ELYSIAN HILLS 1981
Fabric and thread, 25" x 32"
Private collection

THE RED HOUSE 1986, fabric and thread, 25½" x 34½"
Artist's collection

By the mid-'80s, I had undertaken several landscape commissions of specific locations. My
research required meticulous drawing and photographing of the exact and recognizable features of
each place. For *The Red House*, I recorded the
building as it appeared in all four seasons before
choosing to portray it in winter.

The Windham Hill Inn proved to be an architec-
turally challenging structure with its multiple
wings, roof angles, and balconies. Its windy
hilltop location was best expressed through the
dancing lines of foliage.

THE WINDHAM HILL INN 1987, fabric and thread, 25" x 31"
Collection of Pat and Grigs Markham

(Top)
QUEEN OF HEARTS 1980
Fabric and thread, 33" x 26"
Collection of Bern Friedelson

(Bottom left)
QUEEN OF SPADES (first version)
1980, fabric and thread, 33" x 26"
Collection of Michael Scott

(Bottom right)
CARNIVAL QUEEN 1981
Fabric and thread, 30" x 19"
Collection of Gianna Dorman

(Opposite)
CASTLE QUEEN 1981
Fabric and thread, 32" x 22"
Artist's collection

Periodically I have dreams that will bug me until I act on them. I started *Queen of Spades* and *Queen of Hearts* after dreaming about them for three nights. For fifteen months beginning in 1980, I built a series of fifteen pieces based on playing cards. At first these traditional, suited queens remained flat, on the surface, and decorative. In studying the history of tarot cards, I followed several theories about their evolution into the modern playing-card deck. I expanded my vocabulary and constructed more symbolic pieces such as *Carnival Queen* and *Castle Queen*.

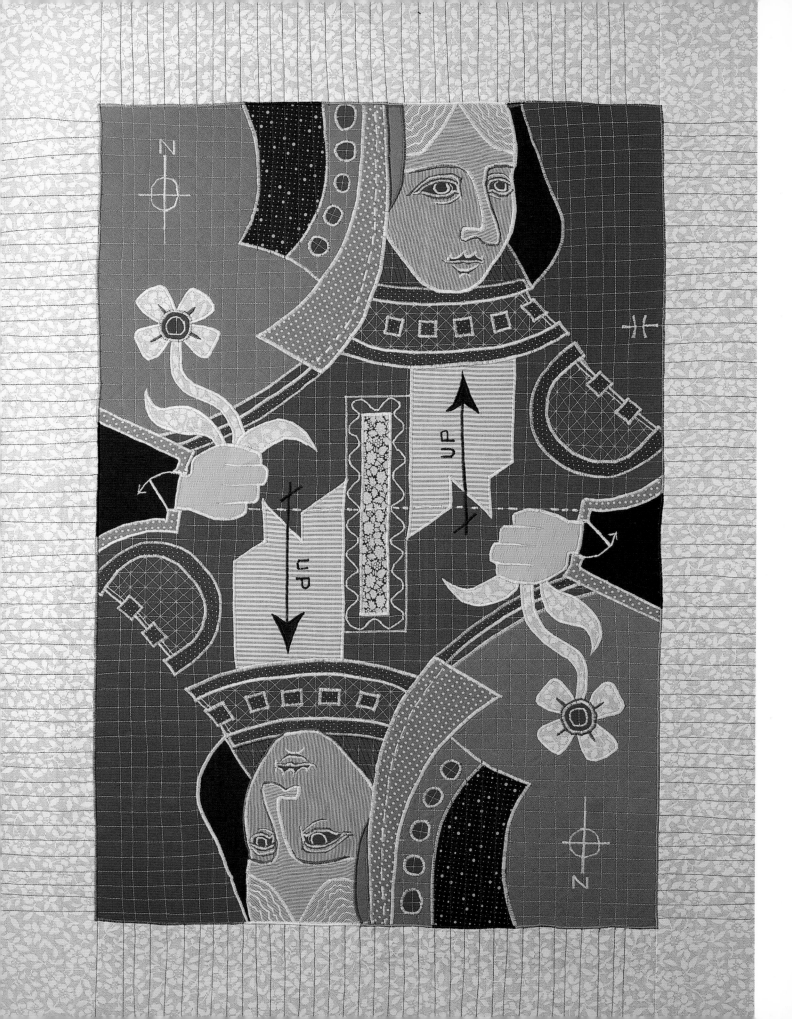

ANNA 1981
Fabric and thread
20½" x 16½"
Private collection

Blueprint of a Queen was different; she was a swing piece. In her face I saw the possibility of a more modeled countenance and a deeper psychological presence. A swing piece is a special work that inspires the next step, a new series, or another direction. Now I learn to recognize when I am having a fascination with a certain work.

(Opposite)
BLUEPRINT OF A QUEEN 1981
Fabric and thread, 32" x 24"
Artist's collection

I have to keep looking at it. By paying attention, the work itself will communicate what is needed next. It has questions, it has answers, and it has energy. Several times in the past, I have sold work without listening to its whole story or to my heart. Today I hang onto a work, at least through that period when it's actively being a swing piece.

Following my predisposition toward representational work, I sensed the need for a shift after completing *Blueprint of a Queen*. I began to draw directly from the people around me. *Anna* exhibits an early modeling attempt using solid-colored fabrics similar to the queens.

STEVE 1981, fabric and thread, 16½" x 13½"
Artist's collection

Within the same month, I started a piece based on Steve. Being a woodworker at the time, Steve is shown with a pencil in his pocket. Using tiny prints and textures, I discovered how accurately I could model his features—the transitions between fabrics were abrupt, yet the pointillistic effect was promising.

These preliminary experiences left me determined to find models for my queenly faces. I contacted Sandy Ware, the Activities Director of a nearby nursing home, Linden Lodge, and asked if I could come in and draw people. I never went back to the queens. To this day I am pulled by my series on elders, by all issues on aging, and by how age-related issues impact the way we live.

Also at that time the famine in Ethiopia did compel me to look at my queens and to question their relevancy. My art calls for a greater meaning than the playfulness, beauty, and symbolism of the queens. I feel the need to connect my work directly to my community.

THE STRAW HAT AGAIN 1983, fabric and thread, 21" x 17"
Collection of Jeff Baird

PEARL OF WISDOM 1984, fabric and thread, 10" x 10"
Private collection

There is an active, vital dialogue between artist
and artwork. This is the big mystery where art
is connected with creation. Initially I hesitated
to name my work process, to understand it, or to
have a dialogue, believing that that activity might
diminish its subconscious development. Instead
I have learned that I can't hurt the unknown.
That as much as I claim of the unknown, there
will always be vast material that will be unreach-
able and unknowable.

With great care I honor the time that it takes to look at a piece. Half of my time in the studio is spent actively cutting, pinning, sewing, or manipulating the fabric. The other half is spent looking. This is serious looking with my eyes moving across the surface of the fabric. I am finding my way toward knowing what the next step is, what it is that I have done, and what I am about to accomplish. This time of questing and assessing turns looking into seeing.

Listening to what I am saying—hearing my internal communication—is the beginning of finding my voice. Equally important is listening to my dreams upon waking and to my daydreams when showering or driving. If a vision of a work comes knocking three times, I pay attention to that inner voice, make sketches or notes, and pursue it. It takes courage to go after glimpses. I have a problem with, "Oh, aren't you lucky that you're so gifted, and you can do this work." It is work! We are all gifted, but using the gift is the relevant part.

Beyond looking, beyond glimpses and dreams, there is *staying power,* which is having the tenacity to see a project through to its greatest degree of evolution. I see in myself a willingness to progress halfway, but not to push a project to complete resolution. I know that the process is not always going to feel comfortable. Starting is particularly troublesome for me, although uncomfortable spots occur all along the path of art-making. It is natural to feel antagonized by a piece or to feel a strong negative or positive charge. This excitement can throw me off, but I am willing to step past it and continue to work whether the energy is there or not. I don't believe in waiting for the muse; I believe in putting myself in her path.

The Last Year

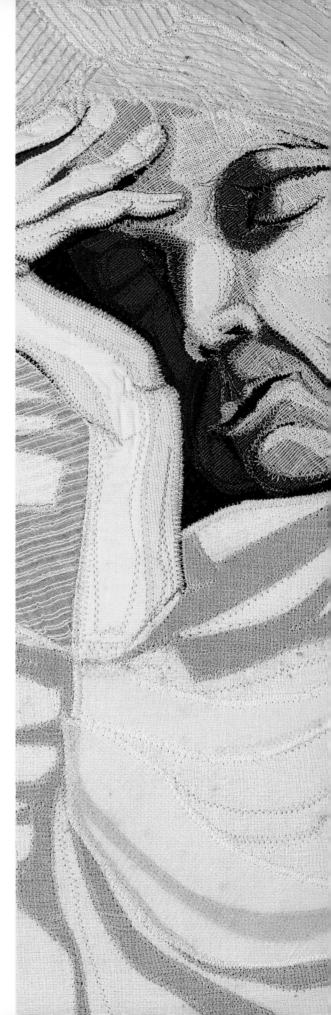

My focus on aging, death, and dying began as I drew elders at Linden Lodge. In stumbling upon this rich world, I realized that I had no image of myself growing old. I gave no importance to aging, or to the framework of living my full life and dying of a full life. What age would I be when I died? Did I assume immortality? Even these questions had missed me.

For answers, I looked back upon my early childhood training in public schools during the '50s, where we were taught to "duck and cover" at the sound of a siren. My whole generation was trained to get under their school desks, bury their heads under their arms to avoid flying glass, and close their eyes so that they wouldn't be blinded. Bomb drills occurred on a regular basis in our schools, along with fire drills. The message was clear; your life and your world could end in a flash.

Throughout my childhood I had dreams of melting and turning to ash. These fears stayed buried until my late thirties when I saw "The Atomic Cafe," a film montage of documentary footage, newsclips, and cartoons from the '50s. Material that had been subliminal in my mind then resurfaced, from bomb shelters to cartoon turtles singing "duck and cover."

For all these years I had not carried a vision of myself as an elder. Around me was an entire society with no sense of aging, and living as if there was no tomorrow. We have no thought of this planet lasting past our individual deaths. Our collective death vision is based on the myth of the total annihilation of our planet. There is little consideration for future generations or their needs, and little hope for the survival of the planet.

As I sat and drew people in the nursing home, again it came to me: I never thought I would grow old. Through witnessing these elders with my pencil, fabric, and thread, I was seeing my own hopes for the future, as well as the planet's possibilities, for the first time.

ANGEL 1985
Fabric and thread, 12" x 10"
Collection of Lillian Farber

Angel is one of my earliest visualizations about the approach of death. To increase the sense of opposites, I used fabric backs and fronts, and opaques and sheer silks, which underline the juxtapositions of her strength and fragility, her dark and light aspects.

Imagining the natural life-span is an antidote to counter all of the visions of violent death and dying out-of-sequence. Today we are haunted by equally numbing devastations, including AIDS, terrorism, ozone depletion, and earth pollution. My imagery of aging counters these horrific catastrophes by elevating the miracle of life. If we can expect a complete life span and a timely death, we can envision a natural life, and a way of being on this planet that isn't destructive.

In one of Don Juan's trilogies is a tale about putting Death over your left shoulder, and looking at every decision in your life with Death as your advisor. This is having both sides of the coin: knowing the miracle of life by contemplating the miracle of death.

My work with elders in the nursing homes has led me directly to Hospice. Hospice is a program that trains volunteers to care for the terminally ill and to assist their primary caregivers. The volunteer workshop helped me develop a spiritual and more open approach to confronting the issues that came bubbling up as a result of looking at and describing aging, death, and dying. Our society does not prepare us for death and rarely speaks of it in a positive, constructive manner. Taboo and silence surround death unless it is violent death. We have an enormous amount of exposure through television and movies to drive-by shootings and stray bullets, to the syndrome of explosions and flying bodies.

DRAWING OF M.F. 1987
Graphite on paper, 16" x 14"
Artist's collection

LAYERS 1990, fabric and thread, 15" x 13"
Artist's collection

Nothing comes close to honoring the profound stages that one moves through toward a natural death with age. As I progressed from "The Elders" to the issues of dying, Hospice provided me with a forum for the feelings of inevitability, both positive and negative. We have all taken our first breath, and we are all going to take our last breath. In considering our own death, we have a chance to consider our own life. This is the dialogue of my work, and this is the dialogue I go through when I'm working.

"The Last Year" is a series of nine fabric and thread works that visualize the final year of a woman's life. She was eighty-nine when we became friends. I had a sense of urgency about witnessing her experience with pencil, crayon, and chalk.

Several months into the drawings, I translated two of them into fabric and brought them to her. Because she was an artist, she thoroughly enjoyed seeing them. At this point, I wasn't aware that they were the beginning of a series.

SIDEWAYS 1990, fabric and thread, 14½" x 13"
Artist's collection

*Now that the harvest is gathered and you stand in the autumn
of your life, your oar is no longer a driving force carrying you
over the oceans of your inner and outer world, but a spirit of
discriminating wisdom, separating moment by moment the
wheat of life from the chaff, so that you may know in both
wheat and chaff their meaning and their value in the pattern
of the universe.*
                                                    HELEN LUKES

IN BETWEEN 1990, fabric and thread, 14" x 13"
Artist's collection

What has happened has happened. The water
You once poured into the wine cannot be
Drained off again, but
Everything changes. You can make
A fresh start with your final breath.

BERTOLT BRECHT

DRAWING OF M.F. 1988, graphite on paper, 14" x 17"
Artist's collection

Over the course of that year, it became an effort
for her just to breathe and to be in her body.
At a certain point, I walked in and found her
using oxygen. Instead of canceling our session
because of my own discomfort and unfamiliarity
with tubes and oxygen tanks, I asked, "Would
you like me to stay? Would you like me to draw
you today?" She was very smart, she said, "Of
course, sit down" knowing that I'd be there at
least two hours. While I drew her, I realized that
she was finding comfort receiving the oxygen, as
she curled herself around the tube in an almost
fetal position.

LATE MAY 1990, fabric and thread, 15" x 13"
Artist's collection

Later in the course of that year, she breathed on
her own, not needing the support of the oxygen.

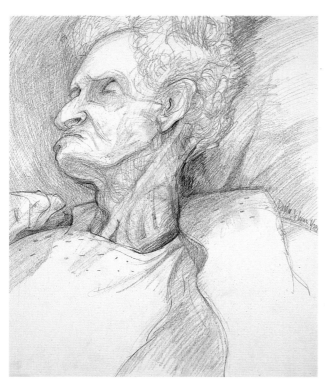

DRAWING OF M.F. 1988
Graphite on paper, 17" x 14"
Artist's collection

On other visits she was visibly uncomfortable, yet brave, incredibly powerful, and present. She internally let go of things by either forgiving others or forgiving herself. Her process was a complex one of shedding and surrendering. Sometimes I would hold her hand and keep drawing with my other hand. In witnessing her particular story, I recognized a universal current running beneath it: I could imagine myself in this place.

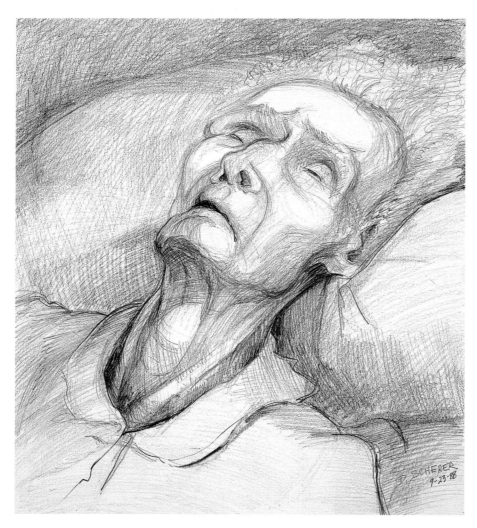

DRAWING OF M.F. 1988
Graphite on paper, 16" x 14"
Artist's collection

RELEASE 1990, fabric and thread, 14" x 13"
Artist's collection

When she died, I put aside the drawings and I grieved. It took two years before I touched them again. With time, I began to see the drawings for what they are—a visual story of her final year. Eventually I translated each drawing into fabric and thread, and this body of work became "The Last Year."

Now "The Last Year" has traveled to sites throughout the States and to Montreal, where it succeeded in crossing verbal and language boundaries. One viewer saw himself in the work, and then he imagined his own daughter at ninety. With my work, he was able to cross the lines of gender as well as generations. "The Last Year" offers an opportunity to start this internal conversation.

LISTEN 1990, fabric and thread, 24½" x 21"
Artist's collection

EXTENSION 1994
Fabric and thread
44" x 30"
Artist's collection

In 1994 I started to work again with the same drawing that inspired *Release* and *Listen*. This version grew to a tremendous size in spite of my own limitations with time and space. I had no intention of building her upper body, bed sheets, or hand. At the finished angle, she appears to be floating right off the pillow.

DRAWING OF L.T. 1995, graphite on paper, 17" x 14"
Artist's collection

In March 1995, I did a series of drawings of a neighbor on her deathbed. She had been a friend and mentor for years, and I felt completely touched by her spirit when I was there. I felt blessed to be in her presence, and though she would regularly doze off, she knew I was there drawing her. I was not there at her death, but I heard later from the nurses that it was a most beautiful and gentle passing. It was the kind of death that we don't hear about.

UNFOLDING 1995, fabric and thread, 17" x 16"
Collection of Michael and Elisabeth Kalogris

In *Unfolding*, I remember the still place that I had witnessed in her. The deep keyhole shadow behind her hand anchors the swirling movement surrounding her. When someone dies, I feel like I have been left behind. However, if I dwell on this abandonment, or the fear of the unknown, I miss the sheer magnitude of the moment. There is a bliss involved in turning from material form to spirit. By disregarding death, our society disregards the intensity and preciousness of life.

The arts provide a marvelous entrée into these worlds. We do not have to avert our eyes. The work of art invites close inspection and takes responsibility for propriety, all the while keeping us focused on larger questions of human decency. The artist or writer leads us beyond the physical, beyond even the psychological, to wander through existential and humanistic realms.

SANDRA L. BERTMAN

The Elders

SISTERS, TOO 1992, fabric and thread, 23" x 18", from *Threads of Experience* (Papier-Mache Press, 1996), collection of Alan Solomont

THE SISTERS 1991
Fabric and thread
31" x 33"
Private collection

As a child growing up on Old Sleepy Hollow Road in upstate New York, I had neighbors who were my elders and mentors. Taking me under their wing, they would teach me how to crochet, make a pie, or plant bulbs. We are blessed to have people in our lives who have shared their gifts with us. One woman owned an amazing collection of dolls from around the world, and she would systematically tell me their histories. I would also visit two sisters, who lived further down the road, always finding them curiously delighted in my presence. I can remember their faces, their shelves of ancient books and the bright windows, the tea they served me, and our unique connection. Their curiosity about who I was, what I was thinking, and what I was doing lit up my own inner voice and my own consciousness. I felt special and gave myself recognition because of their recognition.

More recently, two sisters, who lived independently into their eighties, became my models in every respect. Again, I found in them a sense of sheer delight; everyday was a gift and each moment was a pleasure to be savored. One sister's ability to garden was impressive; the other sister nurtured the townsfolk as well as myself. She recognized me for my art-making and for my mothering. I can still hear her voice on the phone, calling to congratulate my child who made the honor list, or promising to clip the newspaper article that mentioned my work in a show. Receiving this nourishment from my home base inspired several visions including *The Sisters* and *Sisters, Too* that honor our interdependence.

(Top)
EVA HOLT 1982
Graphite on paper, 23" x 17"
Artist's collection

(Bottom left)
EVA (Detail) 1982
Fabric and thread, 35" x 25"
Collection of Margery Feldberg

(Bottom right)
EVA'S DREAM 1987
Fabric and thread, 33" x 27"
Collection of Hilary
and Marvin Fletcher

(Opposite)
EVA'S ALMA MATER 1988
Fabric and thread, 28" x 24"
Collection of Stella
and Arnold Herzog

64

One of my favorite models, Eva, was profoundly deaf and "hard" of sight. My communication with her thrived on a nonverbal level. She is the basis for a series including *Eva, Eva's Alma Mater,* and *Eva's Dream.* Being very much at ease in her body, her presence emanated from a deep place. I felt privileged to draw from her essence.

With a great sense of humor about her situation, she frequently pointed out that I was extremely smart having had three children. She said, "I was too lazy; I had none." She was a schoolteacher and had worked tirelessly all her life. In her thinking, it came to the point where she needed to be in a nursing home because she had no children to take care of her. It was that simple.

STORIES 1986, fabric and thread, 21" x 21"
Collection of Frank and Sharron Kropa

While I am sitting with, listening to, and drawing a particular person, I am aware that I want to make that individual universal. In essence, my works are not portraits. I capture the likeness of my models, but that is not important in and of itself. Quickly my titles shifted to descriptive words. No longer are my works identified by specific names because I want others to bring their own experience, reaction, and dialogue to that piece. This spirit guided me toward giving the title *Stories* to a work based on a graphite drawing of Gertrude. The title refers to the page on her lap, and how she is looking up in remembrance. She is within herself, listening.

GERTRUDE (Detail) 1982
Graphite on paper, 23" x 17"
Artist's collection

WITH PATCHES 1992, fabric and thread, 29½" x 19½"
Private collection

In 1992, I again used the drawing of Gertrude for the colorfully charged piece, *With Patches*. While empathizing strongly with her, it is the patchwork doll in her lap that forcefully grabs my attention. Throughout my childhood, my mother read extensively to me, my sister, and my two brothers, from all of the Oz books (written by L. Frank Baum and illustrated by John R. Neill). Of their entire parade of wild characters, I powerfully connected with Scraps from *The Patchwork Girl of Oz*. When I in turn read this story to my own children, I resolved to build the doll for my daughters Gianna, Corina, and Sarenna. After all those years, Patches came to life—a lanky quilted heroine, full of freedom and movement.

I find that working with family members tends to be therapeutic and ultimately healing. Using drawings, watercolors, and photographs of my father, I continue to build a series that witnesses our relationship and the development of our friendship. In 1987 the piece, *My Father* began the series which spans ten years to the most recently completed, *Unsaid*.

MY FATHER 1987
Fabric and thread, 13" x 11"
Collection of Cicely Aikman
and Fred F. Scherer

TO REFLECT 1993
Fabric and thread, 9" x 8"
Collection of Bill
and Linda Green

UNSAID 1997, fabric and thread, 11" x 10"
Collection of Mary Curzan

RADIANT SPAN 1997, fabric and thread, 28" x 25"
Artist's collection

In *Radiant Span* I worked from a 1949 photograph of my grandmother and myself. Nana is 49; I am five years old. Her sunny backyard, the size of a postage stamp, became my first tie to the natural world—the great outdoors. Everything there was sun-drenched and yellow. In that little garden she grew lily of the valley and an enormous lilac bush. I remember sitting in the foliage, in the perfume of the lilac, and singing at the top of my lungs.

By phone and by mail I shared memories of Nana with my mother, aunts, and uncle. I searched through the window of Nana's photo, and through the window of my own heart, to comprehend where our spirits were back in 1949. By looking intently at the photograph, I began to perceive who she was, what our alliance was, and what we were doing at that time in our lives.

Over the months, the right colors slowly fell together. The background fabrics, the brilliant yellows and the honeycomb pattern, were crucial to expressing the nature of a beehive and of nurturing. I can see how my grandmother is powerful in her protectiveness of my energy, yet knows how to reach and hold me without suppressing me. After spreading out the fabrics on the floor of my studio, two months passed before I could approach the first cut. In building this piece, I commemorate her spirit and I honor how she introduced me to gardening and nature.

A view of another relationship occurs in an earlier work, *Oma*, in which a caring grandmother holds her sleeping grandchild. The baby is clothed in a green flowing robe. Both of their heads have subtle halos fashioned from the netting that blows in the wind behind them. As I developed these figures, the delicate quality of the child emerged, while the grandmother's concern grew ominously. At a certain point in my mind, the grandmother became Mother Nature cradling the baby Planet Earth gently back to health. In both *Oma* and *Radiant Span*, the grandmothers and their grandchildren evoke the intergenerational connection and the significance of that connection to our survival.

My work on elders is represented most extensively in my series on mentors. Since 1981 this series continues to grow and encompasses over two hundred and sixty images. These mentors are older friends who inspire me to create images that are honest. They are models in the sense that I not only want to portray them, but also wish to become like them, to be a mentor myself.

OMA 1990, fabric and thread, 22" x 18½"
Collection of Paul S. Rhodes, M.D.

Gallery

FIRST GLIMPSE 1995
Fabric and thread, 7" x 6"
Collection of Dr. Jill Mortensen

WATERSIDE 1993
Fabric and thread, 11" x 10"
Collection of Alan Gartner
and Dorothy Kerzner Lipski

ENVISAGE 1993
Fabric and thread, 19" x 17"
Collection of Ethel and Martin Simon

(Top left)
FULL MEASURE 1995
Fabric and thread
10" x 8"
Collection of Karol
and Alan Dow

(Top right)
SHEER SUBSTANCE 1996
Sheer fabric and thread
11" x 9"
Private collection

(Bottom)
ENTERING 1996
Fabric and thread, 9" x 8"
Left Bank Gallery;
Wellfleet, Massachusetts

(Top left)
THE CROWN 1993
Fabric and thread, 10" x 9"
Collection of Irving Zaretsky

(Top right)
CHANGE OF KEY 1996
Fabric and thread, 9" x 8"
Collection of Suzan Fine

(Bottom)
INWARD TURN 1997
Fabric and thread, 11" x 10"
Collection of Beryl
and Jordan Benderly

(Top)
SIENNA 1992
Fabric and thread, 22" x 19"
Collection of Deborah
and Mark Simon

(Bottom)
GIFTS 1996
Fabric and thread, 32" x 54"
St. Mary's Foundation;
Rochester, New York

PINK KITCHEN 1987
Fabric and thread, 29" x 27"
Sarah's Circle, Washington, DC:
Gift of Elizabeth O'Connor

SAINT 1992
Fabric and thread, 7" x 6",
from *Return of the Great
Goddess*, (Stewart, Tabori
& Chang Publications, 1997)
Collection of Roman
and Maria Kozak

POISED 1992
Fabric and thread, 8½" x 7½"
Collection of Marcia Hammond

(Top left)
PART ONE 1994
Fabric and thread, 8" x 7"
Collection of Sheila Willson

(Top right)
PART TWO 1997
Fabric and thread, 16" x 14"
Collection of Karen Biedler Alexander

(Bottom)
CROSSINGS 1995
Fabric and thread, 7" x 6"
Collection of Laura Morrissette

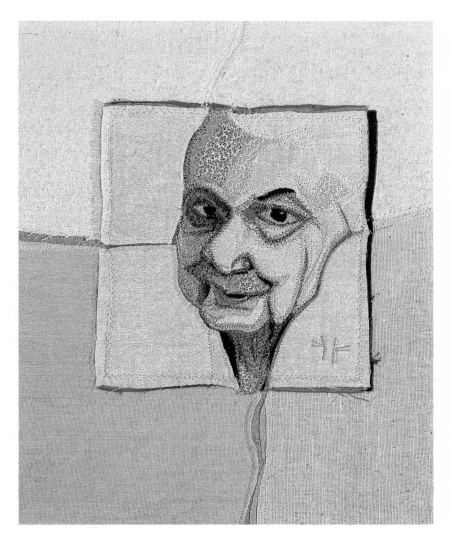

(Top left)
TAKING TIME 1994
Sheer fabric and thread, 9" x 8"
Collection of Janet Bardzik

(Top right)
GOLDEN BUDDHA 1996
Fabric and thread, 6" x 7"
Collection of Elizabeth Rutherford

(Bottom)
WORLD VISION 1997
Paper, fabric, and thread, 10" x 9"
Artist's collection

WITH REGARD 1993
Fabric and thread, 10" x 9"
Private collection

GOLDEN SOURCE 1996
Fabric and thread, 11" x 10"
Private collection

AUGUST SHADE 1994
Fabric and thread, 11" x 10"
Collection of Charlotte
and Richard Thalin

EARTH 1992
Fabric and thread, 10½" x 9"
Collection of Michaeleen
and Edward T. Smith

(Top)
TAKING NOTE 1996
Fabric and thread, 13" x 11"
Collection of Hugh Loebner

(Bottom left)
SUNPOINT 1994
Fabric and thread, 11" x 10"
Collection of Robert
and Pamela Amer

(Bottom right)
INFUSED 1995
Fabric and thread, 9" x 8"
Artist's collection

PAUSE 1992
Fabric and thread, 9" x 8"
Collection of Irving Zaretsky

RECOGNITION 1992, fabric and thread, 10" x 9"
The Baltimore Museum of Art, Maryland

Hands

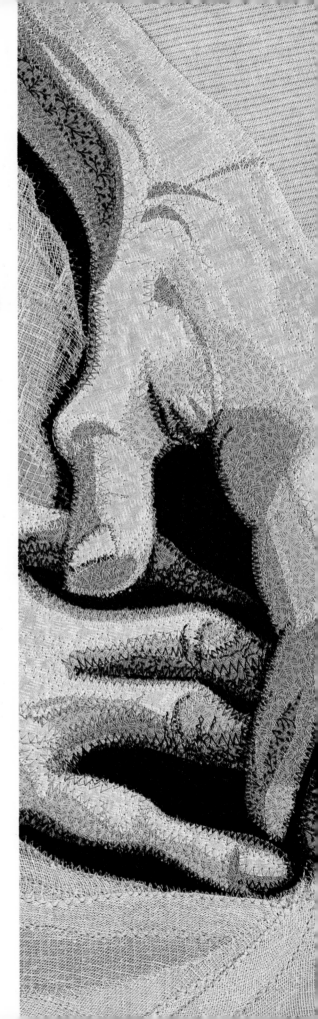

NEW MOON CUP 1993, fabric and thread, 10" x 9"
New Moon Gallery; Salisbury, Maryland

FORMATION 1994, fabric and thread, 11" x 10"
Collection of Tom and Linda Robinson-Hidas

Hands, like laughter, distinguish us as human. Hands, like faces, acquire their own personalities over time. By gaining calluses, odd crooks, or bends, our hands convey information about who we are, how we work, and how we live. People look and say, "I know whose hands those are." They may be mistaken, but they're recognizing something. Hands are more universal than the head, allowing the viewer to read into a set of hands their own experience and their own stories.

I see hands in a relationship to each other. There is always an exchange between left and right, a conversation between partners. In my portraits, hands are positioned in conjunction with a head, such as a single hand cradling a chin, or fingers poised on a cheek. You can read about the life of a person from the lines, position, and vitality of their hands. By themselves, these hands are portraits.

The series on hands started when I realized that I was ignoring them in my work—not paying clear attention to them because they actually intimidated me. They are intense and complex structures. I would put hands into a piece without focusing on them. I was afraid that I couldn't capture them.

For years I have been drawn to the work of French sculptor Auguste Rodin. In 1994, I visited the Rodin Museum in Paris and was thrilled to see his work in marble. I watched people who were completely transfixed, circulating around Rodin's works, many of which included exquisitely sculpted marble hands.

That experience shifted me into really looking at what I was doing with hands, to isolate them in my work, and to focus on the hands alone—without body or head. When starting, I found out how necessary it was to hang in there and not give up, to work until the hands would feel right. This meant that they didn't have to be anatomically correct, just as long as I had conviction

about their structure. Waiting for that "feel right" place was everything. I found that place with the series on hands.

Both *New Moon Cup* and *Formation* are based on the same model in the same position. I was attracted to the space, or negative areas, in between the palm of the hand and the fingers. The upper and lower hands cup a whole universe. In this deep shadowed area, which was as important as the hands themselves, was a magic that kept calling me. My response in *Formation* was to bring in an electric blue fabric and leave a thin line of it to accentuate the contours. In *New Moon Cup*, the mystery is achieved by the depth of the enclosed shape.

KNOWING HOW 1994, fabric and thread, 17" x 20"
Collection of Annabel D. Edwards

For the piece called *Knowing How*, I went into the Brattleboro Senior Center seeking models to fulfill an image that I had glimpsed in my mind's eye. I was fortunate to find three women who met regularly and quilted together. Their circle of friendship encouraged me to ask if they would pose for me in a circle. They put down their work and joined hands while I stood on a chair and photographed them from a bird's-eye view. The women felt so capable in the way they had formed and held that circle.

In the beginning of constructing this piece, I set the hands against a dark background. Midway through I cut away most of the dark fabric and only preserved the remaining black contour lines. I knew that the womens' strength must be apparent in their interlocking hands, as well as in the negative spaces between them. The central negative space is layered over a light fabric so that it leaps forward.

MY MOTHER'S HANDS

*I think of you in my travels about the city but especially at the end of a long hard day like this one.
I think of your hands (which you once told me you thought were ugly) but which I know are so beautiful.
They have your life written in them; they have been shaped by the earth you have loved. Your hands!
they have dug in the soil, & given it so much nourishment, exactly as much as they have been given in return. They have lived, & been beloved.*

Your hands! I love your hands! Those blue bulgy veins you think are "unattractive" are really the blue streams of the high country. They are your ways of worshipping as you work in the Earth, it is your version of the shaping The Great Spirit does, as you are shaped in return. And so are the very life forces shaped as they work thru you, learning in their turn, &, as it has taken time for this round, this partnership to be formed, so have your hands evolved. It has taken time for them to be distilled, like wine, & to grow, like the roots of trees. Look at the bark of a stone pine or the twisting branches of a madrone. Look at your hands again, & see through my eyes: by God! they have seen all weathers! A baby's hand might be freshly-minted & have its own beauty, but it has no soul, for it takes time for a canyon, or a pair of hands, to grow a soul.

I see you shining through the skin of your hands like the sun inside the leaves of your apple trees.

GEOFFREY BROWN

HARVEST HANDS 1993, fabric and thread, 11" x 9"
Collection of Susan Bailis

Harvest Hands describes a woman who has been working the soil, her interaction with the soil, and the way the earth has formed her hands over the years. To further express this, I worked with the colors of autumn: oranges and burnt sienna. Her hands, though worn and deeply creased, show a thickness and muscularity from work.

In *Harvest Hands* the point of view shifts from that of an outside observer to that of a participant. This view asserts that "these are my hands in my own lap." They are seen from our own perspective—not from across the room. The working photograph was taken from over the model's shoulder.

ALABASTER 1993
Fabric and thread, 11" x 9"
Private collection

In *Alabaster* I used a very subtle palette and challenged myself to work with the drawing and modeling of the hands in light and shade. The strength of this piece is based on that draftsmanship—there is no color to distract. *Light Cover* also works with soft hues and sheer fabrics; the skin is fragile yet the hands are strong.

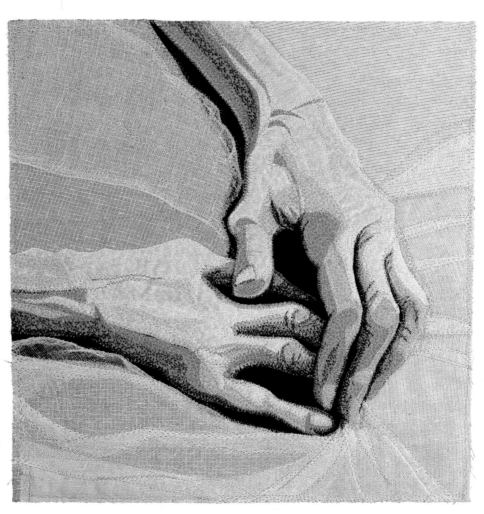

LIGHT COVER 1996
Fabric and thread, 14" x 13"
Collection of Cynthia Boyer

CROSSING BORDERS 1995, fabric and thread, 15" x 13"
Collection of Suzan Fine

Crossing Borders portrays two hands, each reaching out and holding the other tentatively. They are symbolically crossing the lines of gender and difference. The greatest challenge in working with fabric and thread, in using scissors and sewing machine to draw, is the misconception that this medium is stiff and limited, or that these tools are invalid as artists' tools. In *Crossing Borders*, I push the boundaries of what can be done in fiber: I "paint" figuratively in a medium that has not been given credit for its plasticity.

INSIDE OUT 1994
Fabric and thread, 14" x 12"
Collection of Dan Gehan

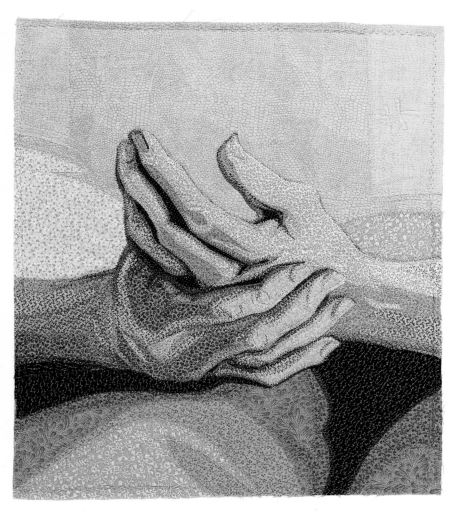

NEW WORLD 1996
Fabric and thread, 13" x 11"
Collection of J. Sawin

Process

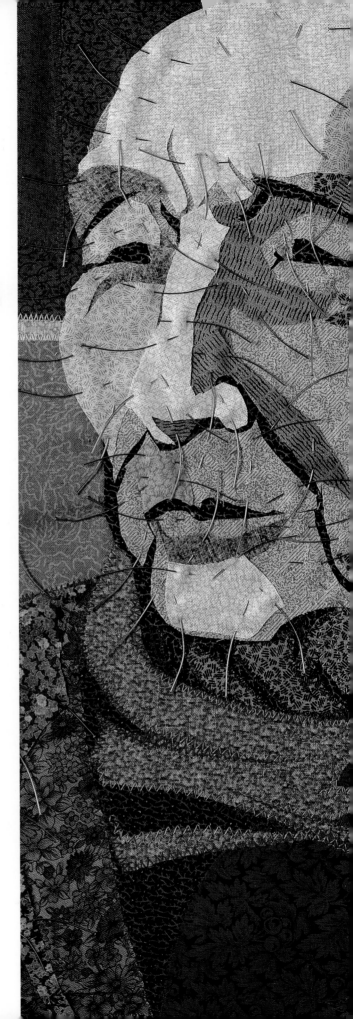

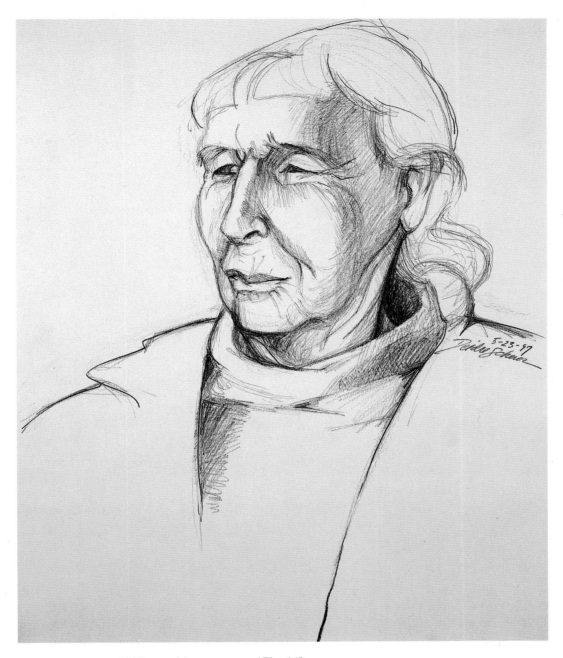

DRAWING OF PAM 1997, graphite on paper, 17" x 14"
Artist's collection

Beginning a piece is the most difficult place
for me. The middle and the ending are nothing
compared to the start of a piece—making that
initial commitment to a specific palette of colors,
a certain figure and emotions. I realize I'll be
contending with my decisions for the full duration
of the project, whether it be a week or seven
months. There is a bit of stagefright involved,
and not letting it stop me is key to accomplishing
anything.

After propping up the drawing of Pam on the
back of my work table, I direct my lights onto it.
I pull my stool over, sit down with a cup of tea,
and begin to gaze at my drawing, considering
my direction and the size, shape, and tone of
the piece.

After several more cups of tea, I have chosen twenty-two different fabrics, and the color spectrum surprises me. Selecting the colors is an emotional choice, although I am sure that the greens and yellows are influenced by my model's love of the forest and the natural world. A range of intense, deep blues and browns will anchor the darkest notes and shadows of the head. All my other color choices cover the medium notes and then proceed into the highlights. By considering the back or reverse side of each fabric, my color range increases twofold. I gather my fabrics in close alignment to the shapes and movements I see in my drawing. The drawing sits clearly visible at my cutting table. It is there for guidance and referral.

The rectangular shape I've chosen for this new work measures thirteen inches high by twelve inches wide. I start with two layers of muslin, which I immediately cover with a soft, mossy green field of fabric. These three layers give bulk and provide stability when sewing.

In the first cutting, I get an abstract understanding of the space. A blue floral for her body and various greens and yellows for the background are roughly cut and moved around for placement. The shoulders and shirt neckline are also cut and positioned. After blocking in the background and the sweep of her shoulders, it is already apparent how she is holding her head. Her attitude is beginning to show. Like the foundation of a house, the piece will rest on this early division of the space.

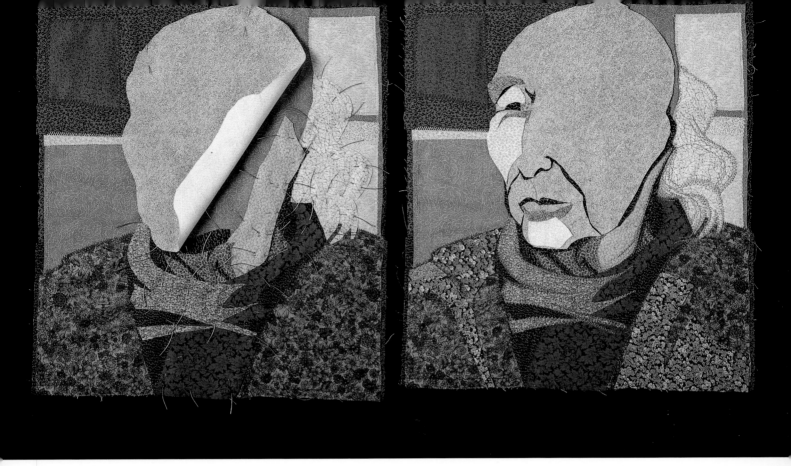

STAGE TWO

Rather than basting, gluing, or bonding, I prefer pinning because it allows for some movement when sewing. Pinning is a slow and tedious process. I use headless straight pins that are 1¼" long and the finest I can find; so fine they've been sorely bent through usage. That thinness allows the unfinished edges of multiple layers of fabric to be pinned without creating enormous ridges or ripples.

Next, I prepare for my second sewing. The first sewing had only fixed the raw edges of the background and body. Now I cut and block in an approximate head shape in order to determine the position of her neck, collar, and hair, as well as the shapes that will fall in the background. Before sewing I will remove the head shape and pin all the new edges meticulously. Drawing with my machine, I stitch over the pins as I go, using

STAGE THREE

a light pressure on the sewing foot and an extra fine needle. I vary the length and width of my zigzag stitch as I capture the raw edges.

Bearing down with a moderately hot iron, I flatten and ease the second sewing which includes the neck and hair. Replacing the head shape, I start to cut the basic structures of the chin, mouth, and nose. The deepest of my brown fabrics has been slipped under those areas, as well as under the right side of her face, her eye, and eyebrow. Lighter fabrics are cut and added along her cheek and chin, replicating the daylight that flowed across her face. Already there are eight layers of fabric in some places.

STAGE FOUR

At this stage, I continue to build with layers of fabric across the nose, and then into the shadows that give shape to the left side of her face. While intently looking at my graphite of Pam, I have directly drawn and cut with my scissors into the lighter fabrics as highlight, the deeper shades as shadow. I have moved across the face, from the bridge of her nose to the highlights on her forehead and into the deeper, darker left side of her face. I have cut away as well as added, so this has been both a subtractive and additive method of building the surface. I end this phase by intricately pinning over the entire surface: this allows me to begin the following work session with sewing. I can see the spirit of this piece coming through.

STAGE FIVE

I spend the whole night drawing with my machine. This includes structural sewing to capture the edges, as well as drawing or oversewing to bring in both highlights and shadows. For the machine-drawing, I use different colors of thread to either blend or sharpen adjoining areas. I slow down to carefully finish her eyes, sometimes moving the needle in and out by hand. The body of her hair is established with several tones of gray and white fabric. Later, stray wisps can be added with heavier lines of white or gray thread. I may eventually change the background that is on the right side of her head in order to achieve a little more contrast.

STAGE SIX

In the early morning hours the birds are chirping and I am still at work. The hair and ear have been pinned and sewn. I have introduced a warm color into the shadows on the left side of her face. Yet becoming increasingly dissatisfied with the greens and the mosses in the background, I carefully replace them with three new fabrics: a dense red-brown, an airy brown, and a mustard yellow. I cut, layer, and pin over the original fabrics and float a little bit of the brown into her blue shirt. It radically changes the color relationships throughout the piece. Now it is time to let the work rest. I will wait and see how that settles with her.

SIGNATURE

This is my signature, my mark, or chop, and it represents my name. At the time when my name had expanded to an inconvenient, great length, I dreamed of this distinctive mark and adopted it. It is a way of claiming all of the names that have been a part of my life.

CLEARING 1997, fabric and thread, 13" x 11"
Collection of Barbara Filner and Harry Rosenberg

The following night, I sew in the final decision on
my background; the brown fabric will cover the
green fabric. With thread I draw additional
highlights around her eyes, forehead, cheek-
bones, and at the corner of her mouth. The
expression lightens up and gains depth all at the
same time. For hours I oversew and draw; I shade
and highlight until I feel her beaming through.
The title *Clearing* comes to mind as it associates
Pam with the forest. I sign this piece in blue.

Publications

(Top)
THE PINK PIG 1985
Fabric and thread, 21" x 15"
(Materialnotes) Collection of Randy
and Corina Willette

(Bottom left)
PATCHES 1985
Fabric and thread, 21" x 15"
(Materialnotes) Collection of Terri Melo

(Bottom right)
RA-TA-TAT CAT 1985
Fabric and thread, 21" x 16"
(Materialnotes) Private collection

CHUGGA-RUM 1985
Fabric and thread, 21" x 15"
(Materialnotes) Artist's collection

Original art becomes more accessible and democratic when made into prints and reproductions. For this reason I feel compelled to put my work out in multiple forms of reproduction, such as book covers, posters, and cards.

During the mid-1980s, Steve and I established our own company, Materialnotes, and began to reproduce my images as cards. We printed two portraits on aging, a set of still-life cards, three angels, and nine children's cards. *Patches* became one of the children's cards, along with the other characters that I had created for my daughters, such as *The Pink Pig*, *Chugga-Rum*, and *Ra-ta-tat Cat*.

IN THE NIGHT TREE
1986, fabric and thread
23" x 18½", (Materialnotes)
Collection of Dorthea Ferone

Of the three guardian angels, *In the Night Tree* became a vision that I worked with repeatedly, as shown in the 1992 *Aerie*. Both the angels and the children's pieces support my desire to reconnect with my own fantasies and spiritual imagination.

AERIE 1992
Fabric and thread, 22" x 17"
Collection of William (Ron) Patsy

TREE 1988
Fabric and thread, 9" x 7½"
Collection of Cicely Aikman
and Fred F. Scherer

TREE ON PAPER 1989
Photogravure, 10" x 9"
(Renaissance Press)
Collection of Carol Cataldo

In 1989, I was determined to make a fine-art print directly from my work. I began by placing my original fabric piece called *Tree*, facedown on a color laser copier. Using semitransparent Mylar® paper, I made black and white copies of the piece. I then took the Mylar copy of *Tree* to my friend and artist, Paul Taylor, who encouraged my ideas.

Paul runs a fine art printing studio, Renaissance Press, across the river in Hinsdale, New Hampshire. Only a handful of printmaking studios have mastered the photogravure process, which is similar to but more arduous than etching. Using photogravure techniques, Paul transferred my Mylar image onto a copper plate from which he pulled several prints. The outcome was *Tree On Paper*, which raised our hopes, yet still lacked clarity because of the loss of detail. I dreamed of a more direct method that would eliminate any extra steps, such as the use of the color laser copier.

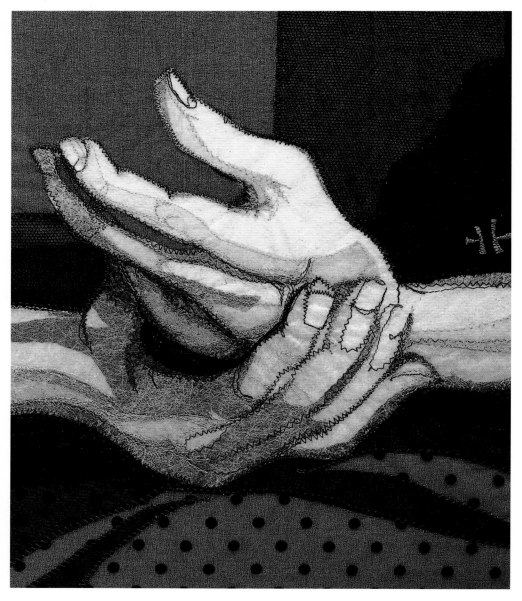

ABOUT ROOTS 1993, sheer fabric and thread, 11" x 9"
Private collection

In 1993, I built an image of a pair of hands, utilizing only sheer fabrics such as silk organza and cotton netting. All my materials were chosen for their translucent or transparent natures.
To view the effects of light, I constantly held the work up to a window or against my light box as I proceeded. The fabrics were cut, precisely layered, and delicately sewn for the sole intent of letting light shine through them and of discerning how the shadows were created. Each thread, each fine filament, and every sewn line became a silhouette of itself.

When making the copper plate for this image, Paul projected light through my sheer fabric piece. The piece was used as a positive to contact-print directly onto the copper plate, which was covered with a light-sensitive gel. That plate was then etched in ferric chloride.

44/300   "ABOUT ROOTS"   Deidre Scherer, 1997

ABOUT ROOTS 1997, limited edition photogravure
11" x 9", (Renaissance Press)

We were ecstatic to see the vivid impressions that were pulled from *About Roots*. My cut fabrics and sewn lines had been translated into ink on paper— textured areas and lines of ink! We believe that no one else has used an original fabric work as the positive for a gravure print. As we move ahead with a limited edition of *About Roots*, our collaboration and experimentation with printmaking continues.

(Top)
MORE 1992
Fabric and thread, 9" x 8"
Cover of *If I Had My Life to Live Over I Would Pick More Daisies*, (Papier-Mache Press, 1992) Artist's collection

(Bottom left)
FREIDA 1984
Fabric and thread, 10" x 10"
Cover of *Another Language,* (Papier-Mache Press, 1988) Collection of Tracy Brogan Cole

(Bottom right)
LAUGHING ROSE 1985
Fabric and thread, 7" x 7"
Cover of *When I Am an Old Woman I Shall Wear Purple,* (Papier-Mache Press, 1987) Collection of Theodora and Stanley Feldberg

114

COUNTERPOINT 1995
Fabric and thread, 11" x 10"
Cover of *Grow Old Along
with Me—The Best Is Yet
to Be*, (Papier-Mache Press,
1996) Artist's collection

Over the years, I am delighted that seven of my
works have become remarkably visible on the
covers of Papier-Mache Press books. *Laughing
Rose* graces the cover of the first anthology, *When
I Am an Old Woman I Shall Wear Purple*, which
has sold one and a half million copies. This book
has been sighted worldwide—from Canada to
India. The most recent anthology, *Grow Old Along
with Me—The Best Is Yet to Be*, features *Counterpoint*, a double portrait on its cover. The presence
of these images helps to fulfill my wish for powerful and positive visual archetypes of aging to enter
our social consciousness.

In the fall of 1996, Sandra Martz of Papier-Mache Press and I collaborated on the book *Threads of Experience*. This edition pairs twenty-five of my images in full-color with poems and essays by twenty-four contemporary writers. In this book, we created a visual tool with an evocative verbal message to help our world more openly discuss aging.

TREASURE 1993, fabric and thread, 11" x 10"
Cover of *Threads of Experience*, (Papier-Mache Press, 1996) Collection of Irwin and Marilyn Scher

Still Life

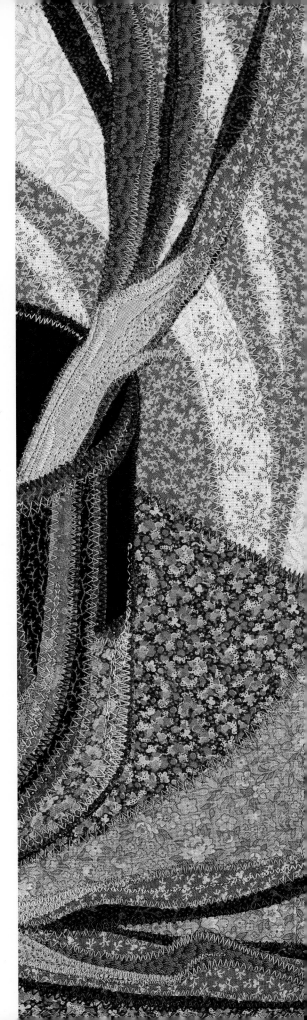

FOR SWEETNESS 1996, fabric and thread, 11" x 10"
Cover of *Like a Summer Peach: Sunbright Poems
and Old Southern Recipes,* (Papier-Mache Press,
1996) The Art & Attic, Redbank, New Jersey

BOUQUET IN GLASS 1987
Fabric and thread, 18" x 14"
Collection of Jeff Baird

During stressful times, I use the still life to help remain centered and to give myself respite. To begin a still life, I passionately arrange and rearrange simple objects: apples, peaches, eggs, or vegetables in combination with a bowl or plate, often laying out fabrics behind as well as under the objects. By sensitively adjusting my lamps, the light hits and describes the shapes by creating highlights and shadows.

PRAYER PLANT 1986
Fabric and thread
14" x 10", (Materialnotes)
Private collection

The three-dimensional placement of objects and light constitutes half the effort, similar to building a sculpture. I concentrate on being there in a moment of truth, seeing every small nuance and hanging onto that sense of presence with urgency. Seeing the exact spatial relationships in the still life, and then dividing the surface plane accordingly, is a mathematical game. Primary decisions are made about how the horizontal lines of the table will dissect the vertical and diagonal elements. Geometrical divisions are chosen for their rhythmic qualities, their surprise, and for their sheer joy. I like to hang the curves and ovals of the bowls and fruit along the spine of this spatial armature. Leaning over these objects, I absorb their existence as I begin to cut and layer the background fabrics.

THREE APPLES 1991, fabric and thread, 10½" x 9"
Collection of Carole Greenbaum

120

TWO GOLDENS 1997, fabric and thread, 11" x 10"
Collection of Dan Gehan

My earlier still-life work displays a sense of fantasy and less of a tie to reality. In *The White Cat*, I allow the spider plant and the pot to loom larger than the cat. A subtle shift occurs between this still life and a piece such as *Cut Apple With Water*. When looking into and through that glass of water, I see a myriad of surprising abstractions. Shadows and reflections appear that are more fantastic than any invention or dream.

The same element of surprise happens in *The Blue Bowl*. Having chosen that shiny, dark bowl, I focus on its blueness, cutting it from bright blue cloth. As I set aside my preconceptions about the color of the bowl, the original blue fabric disappears. Snip by snip, it changes from all blue to all the surrounding colors that reflect, like a mirror, on its shiny surface. In the finished work, only one spot of that original blue remains, caught in a deep shadow right behind the apple.

THE WHITE CAT 1991, fabric and thread, 23" x 21"
Private collection

CUT APPLE WITH WATER 1991
Fabric and thread, 10½" x 9",
from *Like a Summer Peach:
Sunbright Poems and Old
Southern Recipes*, (Papier-Mache
Press, 1996) Collection of Dalene
Barry and Joseph Dean

THE BLUE BOWL 1991, fabric and thread, 10" x 9"
Collection of Marvin and Marianne Guerra

PEACHES 1996, fabric and thread, 11" x 10"
Private collection

Peaches embody a place about creating beauty
that I rarely touch so openly. Their warm, golden
colors with purples running through them, and
their lush, fuzzy surfaces all pose a velvet challenge. And it takes great discipline not to eat
them! By working on something that exquisite,
I find that beauty has a place in my art. If I can
bring someone to pause—as with my portraits—
to stop in awe, and for a moment consider beauty
and beauty in life, I've succeeded.

THREE PEACHES 1997, fabric and thread, 12" x 10"
Private collection

CUT APPLE 1991
Fabric and thread, 10½" x 9"
Private collection

I often cut into apples or peaches, revealing the inner fruit and the seed or pit, but I always wait until the last day, the last possible moment, before cutting them. It becomes a race to finish my work before the apples brown and shrivel up.

SHARING 1996
Fabric and thread, 9" x 8"
Private collection

Leeks are a favorite subject of mine. As a child wandering through the woods behind my house in upstate New York, I would find wild blueberries, black raspberries, and leeks. Today I grow my own leeks and pull them from my garden. During the construction of this series, I had to place the leeks in a bowl of water whenever I stopped working each night in order to keep them fresh and green. I felt connected to the leeks; their forms registered physically on me. It's similar to shutting my eyes after I've been weeding a lot and all I can see are weeds.

Similar to *The Blue Bowl,* a mirror effect occurs in *Leeks in a Cup*. There stands a shiny, dark maroon cup that reflects the world around it while keeping very little of its own color. By cropping the leeks, I catch the feeling of being underneath them, as if inside a forest of tree trunks.

LEEKS IN A CUP 1997
Fabric and thread, 12" x 10"
Collection of Kenneth E. Kehoe

THREE EGGS 1995, fabric and thread, 11" x 10",
from *Like a Summer Peach: Sunbright Poems and
Old Southern Recipes,* (Papier-Mache Press, 1996)
Collection of Mr. and Mrs. Emile Pragoff

EGGS AND LEEKS 1996, fabric and thread, 11" x 10"
Collection of Irwin and Marilyn Scher

Eggs are a remarkably ironic subject matter for fabric medium. There are not too many things that make me think, "I can't do that" in fabric and thread. The eggs come the closest because using a soft material to describe a hard, brittle eggshell is at such odds. To puncture the cloth with a needle and still arrive at "eggness" is inconceivable. I fight to get the perfect egg shape by cutting the fabric in the air, which can take two or three times before succeeding. I also use the shadows cast upon them by both the bowl and the leeks to help define their flawless curves.

Next, my still-life series sends me to our local farm stand, where I spend half an hour going through a basket of jumbo garlic. People eye me curiously as I rotate and carefully study each bulb until I find the most beautiful and interesting ones.

GARLIC #1 1997
Fabric and thread, 7" x 6"
Artist's collection

At home I set the garlic under my lights. Initially thinking of them as simple shapes, I soon discover that their simple shapes and colors are far more complex than I had imagined. Their dry opaque skins soak up the delicate pastel colors that bounce off the surrounding golden mustard fabric. I become speechless, in love with garlic.

GARLIC #2 1997, fabric and thread, 7" x 6"
Collection of Dan Gehan

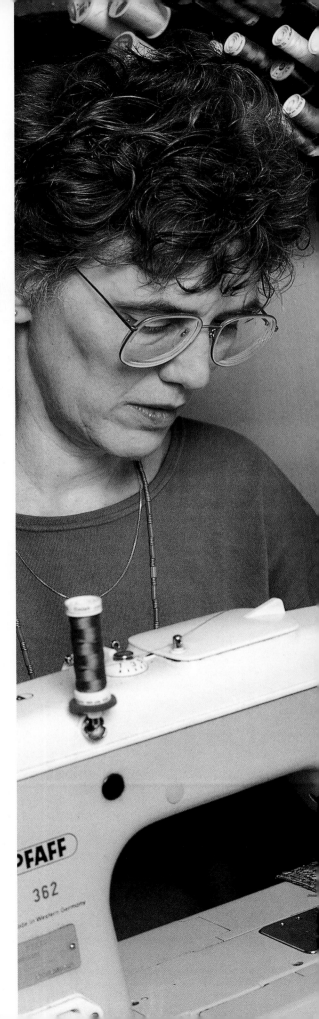

Workspace

Creating a studio is key to creating work. Having control over my workspace is essential to doing my work. When my three daughters were young, we all lived in the 15' x 30' attic room of an old farmhouse. My work area consisted of a single table, several boxes, and some shelves in a cramped corner. Eventually, through a slow evolution, the girls and I expanded into the rest of the house, and I established the attic as my studio.

Such a space means that I can start or stop projects without needing to move them or clean them up. Every day, at all hours, I have complete access and do not have to worry about a guest sleeping there. I can listen to my own music or to my own silence. It is my sacred space.

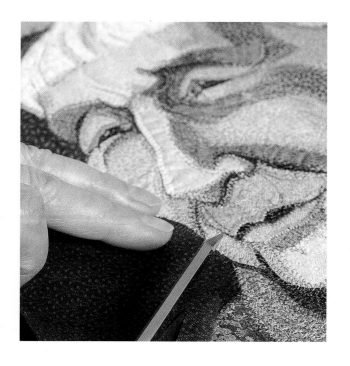

Over time I have developed work stations that include cutting tables, sewing machine tables, both floor and wall viewing areas, ironing board, framing, storage, and business areas. I found comfortable stools and good chairs. My two cutting areas are three-foot high plywood tables that are three-feet deep. With a total of sixteen feet in length, there is enough room for materials to be spread out and for me to engage in simultaneous projects. Fabrics are stored and easily accessible on shelves directly above the tables.

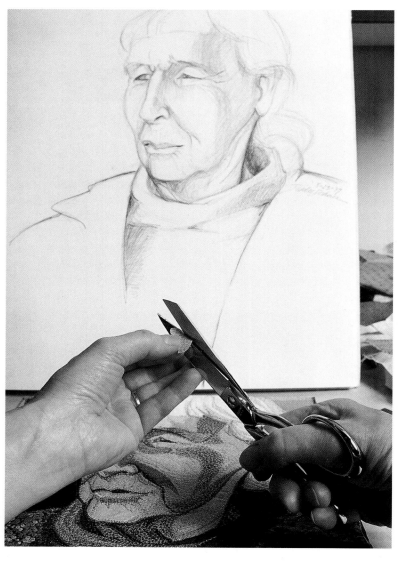

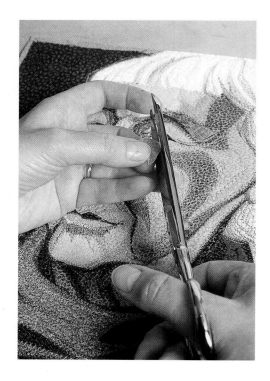

Lighting is important to achieve correct color. I work under full-spectrum bulbs and try to exhibit the work under full spectrum. Although track lighting is ideal, I have relied on a bank of inexpensive clip-on lamps for years. While doing any close detail work, I enjoy flooding the area with several 100-watt light bulbs.

The tools that are part of my space, such as my Pfaff® sewing machine, have to be at a specific height and relationship so that my eyes, arms, and hands are all at comfortable angles. Artists need to take their bodies, positions, and work habits seriously. With tasks such as pinning or sewing, I will take a break every ten minutes or so and gently stretch back in the opposite direction.

A separate office space is a prerequisite to making a commitment to myself as an artist in business. A set of second-hand file cabinets with a door placed across them serves as a business area. Having a word processing program, a mail list program, and a label maker saves time.

As the business of art quickly becomes too complex and too layered, file systems give me a way to create organization in areas where I usually have none. Although I am a paper mountain queen, I have devised a filing system for projects, exhibitions, galleries, magazines, books, grants, other artists, and writers. By putting upcoming dates in a pocket management calendar, I can alert myself to deadlines and details that are tucked into those files. This habit of keeping a calendar frees me from holding the schedule in my mind and gives me more room for creative thinking.

I am representing myself: there is no one else responsible for that. It would be nice to give somebody else that job, but until that is possible, it is imperative to put on that hat and treat it with as much care and originality as I do the work itself. Any presentation I do reflects love and enthusiasm. A third of my studio time is dedicated to business and visibility, which includes updating my résumé, writing newsletters, and creating press releases and kits. I always ask a friend or my husband to do the editing.

The key to good presentation is good visuals. If you can't make perfect slides yourself, use a professional photographer. I credit Jeff Baird, my photographer, for finding the perfect film and balance of light, to bring out the richness and low relief of my fiber surfaces. We record each work in three different formats: color slides, black and white photos, and 4" x 5" color transparencies. Although it is an incredibly tedious detail, labeling slides is part of the presentation quality. I choose to label, carefully, by hand.

Over the years I have subscribed to several arts magazines and newsletters to actively pursue the offerings on their opportunities page. In this way I created exhibition deadlines by entering juried shows, or seeking exhibition opportunities in galleries, museums, or alternative spaces. I have learned to take either rejection or acceptance in stride, to be persistent, and to steadily build on my successes.

Planning a schedule for art-making comes hand-in-hand with having a workspace. If I don't allot time to be in that space, what good does it do me? Being a night owl, I establish five to six studio hours every evening. I block those hours into my calendar and hold onto it more dearly than to a doctor's appointment. I stay on schedule, with or without the muse. It is relatively easy when I am ecstatic and excited about a piece. When the work is difficult, I still get myself into the studio and I sweat. Setting goals, staying on a time line, and being present, whether I feel like it or not, steadily gives me a way to discipline myself. It makes what is impossible, possible.

At various stages in my life there have been different expectations. I now have no children at home and fewer distractions. When my children were young and I was a single parent, I had far less options and less energy, but I did manage to determine a regular time and place to work. Having had to balance studio time with parenting put the appointment book in a different perspective—it was crucial. Even scheduling a short span of time would get me to my workspace.

Another facet of creating studio time is inventing a ritual that delineates that time from the average everyday things in my life. Often I do that by burning incense, playing a game of solitaire, or meditating for a few minutes before engaging in the artwork. It is a mental "clearing of the throat." Even the act of ducking into my room under the low door gives me a sense of entering another world. By setting time and my space apart from everyday life, I confirm the value of my art-making, and the need for it in the world.

The bottom line to being in my own workspace and working on a schedule is getting support from other people. I found support from a women's artist group—in fact, two groups. We meet monthly to help each other dream, set goals, disperse blocks, and move ourselves and our work forward. By developing confidence and courage, I have learned to ask for support outside of my artist groups. It often means a single phone call to say, "I'm about to go into my studio, and I feel a lack of confidence. Please listen to what I'm facing." Asking for pure, open attention helps me clarify my goals and my process.

Being lucid about emotional needs has positively influenced how I approach my financial needs. In the late-80s, I asked Steve to economically support me as a full-time studio artist. He gave me the emotional and financial jump-start I needed to concentrate on my work and to make my work visible. By having the courage to ask friends and family to be allies, I have also learned to present my projects, budgets, and schedules to granting foundations and arts organizations. Artists have always needed support. The arts are not easily sustained by a culture in which consumerism and materialism rule. Western art tradition is a history of the church, the government, and the wealthy families supporting the arts. Funeral marches were written to bury kings, portraits were created to put in the halls of government, and churches adorned their windows and walls with religious teachings.

Like breathing, art is crucial to life. My fabric and thread work is the nonverbal language that connects me to the miracle that is life. Although I use this specific medium to speak of specific human conditions, I am moved by the magic that is moving between the threads. This energy awakens me—art is where the material and spiritual worlds touch.

SELF-PORTRAIT 1997, fabric and thread, 16" x 12"
Artist's collection

About the Author

During the mid-60s, Deidre Scherer studied painting at the Rhode Island School of Design. She developed her distinct narrative approach to fiber while raising her family, and has worked with fabric and thread as her primary medium since the late-70s.

Scherer has addressed the issues of aging and mortality by building a series of images based on elders in her community. In 1994 she received a Fellowship from the Vermont Arts Council.

Scherer's work has been represented in more than 90 shows nationally, including solo exhibitions at the Williams College Museum of Art in Williamstown, MA; the Brattleboro Museum in Brattleboro, VT; the Redding Museum of Art in Redding, CA; the Museum of Fine Arts in Springfield, MA; the Everson Museum of Art in Syracuse, NY; and the Baltimore Museum of Art in Baltimore, MD.

Since the late-80s, Scherer has appeared in the American Craft Council Fairs, the Philadelphia Museum of Art Craft Shows, and in the Smithsonian Craft Shows.

Her pieces were included in "Celebrating the Stitch," which opened in 1992 in Newton, MA, and in "Full Deck Art Quilts," which opened in 1995 at the Renwick Gallery, Smithsonian Institute, National Museum of American Art. Both shows toured extensively and became published books.

Internationally her work has traveled to exhibitions in Canada, England, and Japan. In 1996 she gave the keynote lecture at the National Festival of the Embroiderer's Guild in Durham, England.

Scherer lives with her husband in Vermont, where she works as a full-time studio artist.

PHOTO CREDITS

I would like to thank the following artists for their photographic images from which I have drawn inspiration: John Willis, Hansi Durlach, Rosalie Illingworth, Jane Gattlin, James E. Powers, Ann Zane Shanks, Mara Lavitt, Rick Burt, Karen Thalin, Lucy Fradkin, Arthur Bacon, and Nancy Burgess. I give special thanks to Jeff Baird for brilliantly photographing my work over the years.

Bibliography

PUBLICATIONS

Baum, L. Frank. *The Patchwork Girl of Oz*. Chicago, IL: The Reilly & Lee Co. Publishers, 1913.

Bertman, Ph.D., Sandra L. *Facing Death: Images, Insights and Interventions*. Bristol, PA: Taylor & Francis, 1991.

Brown, Geoffrey. *Road of the Heart Cave*. Newton, MA: Thrown to the Winds Press, 1984.

Busch, Gunter, and Liselotte von Reinken, eds. *Paula Modersohn-Becker: The Letters and Journals*. Arthur S. Wensinger and Carole Clew Hoey, eds. & trans. New York: Taplinger Publishing Company, 1983.

Cameron, Jean. *Time to Live, Time to Die*. Hantsport, Nova Scotia: Lancelot Press, 1982.

Cameron, Julia. *The Artist's Way: A Spiritual Path to Higher Creativity*. New York: The Putnam Publishing Group, 1992.

Castaneda, Carlos. *Tales of Power*. New York: Simon & Schuster, 1974.

Castaneda, Carlos. *The Teachings of Don Juan: A Yaqui Way of Knowledge*. New York: Ballantine Books, 1986.

Cowart, Jack, and Juan Hamilton, essays. Sarah Greenough, annotations. *Georgia O'Keeffe: Art and Letters*. National Gallery of Art, Washington. Boston: New York Graphic Society Books; Little, Brown and Company, 1987.

Crawford, Tad. *Legal Guide for the Visual Artist*. New York: Allworth Press, 1989.

Durlach, Hansi, photos. *The Short Season of Sharon Springs*. Stuart M. Blum, text. Ithaca and London: Cornell University Press, 1980.

Edwards, Betty. *Drawing on the Right Side of the Brain*. Los Angeles: Jeremy P. Tarcher, 1979.

Elkind, Sue Saniel. *Another Language*. Watsonville, CA: Papier-Mache Press, 1988.

Farley, Blanche Flanders, and Janice Townley Moore, eds. *Like A Summer Peach: Sunbright Poems and Old Southern Recipes*. Watsonville, CA: Papier-Mache Press, 1996.

Flam, Jack. *Matisse on Art*. Berkeley and Los Angeles: University of California Press, 1995.

Fowler, Margaret, and Priscilla McCutcheon. *Songs of Experience*. New York: Ballantine Books, 1991.

Graphic Artists Guild, Inc. *Pricing & Ethical Guidelines*. New York: 1994.

Hills, Patricia. *Alice Neel*. New York: Harry N. Abrams, Inc. Publishers, 1983.

James, Michael. *Michael James: Studio Quilts*. Neuchatel: editions Victor Attinger, Massachusetts: Whetstone Hill Publications, 1995.

Kallir, Jane, Essay. *Paula Modersohn-Becker: Germany's Pioneer Modernist*. New York: Galerie St. Etienne, 1983.

Kollwitz, Hans, ed. *The Diary and Letters of Kaethe Kollwitz*. Richard and Clara Winston, trans. Evanston, IL: Northwestern University Press, 1988.

Kübler-Ross, M.D., Elizabeth. *Death Is Of Vital Importance: On Life, Death, and Life After Death*. Barrytown, NY: Station Hill Press, 1995.

Llewellyn, Nigell. *The Art of Death: Visual Culture in the English Death Ritual c.1500–c.1800*. London: Reaktion Books Ltd., 1991.

Martz, Sandra Haldeman, ed. *When I Am an Old Woman I Shall Wear Purple*. Watsonville, CA: Papier-Mache Press, 1987.

Martz, Sandra Haldeman, ed. *If I Had My Life To Live Over I Would Pick More Daisies*. Watsonville, CA: Papier-Mache Press, 1992.

Martz, Sandra Haldeman, ed. *Grow Old Along with Me—The Best Is Yet to Be*. Watsonville, CA: Papier-Mache Press, 1996.

O'Keeffe, Georgia. *Georgia O'Keeffe*. New York: The Viking Press, 1976.

Painter, Charlotte, text, and Pamela Valois, photography. *Gifts of Age*. San Francisco: Chronicle Books, 1985.

Pierce, Sue, and Verna Suit. *Art Quilts: Playing with a Full Deck*. San Francisco: Pomegranate Artbooks, 1994.

Prelinger, Elizabeth, essays. Hildegard Bachert and Alessandra Comini. *Kathe Kollwitz*. National Gallery of Art, Washington. New Haven & London: Yale University Press, 1992.

Ringgold, Faith. *We Flew Over the Bridge: The Memoirs of Faith Ringgold*. New York: Bulfinch Press; Little, Brown and Company, 1995.

Rosenberg, Judith Pierce, ed. A *Question of Balance: Artists and Writers on Motherhood*. Watsonville, CA: Papier-Mache Press, 1995.

Rosinsky, Therese Diamand. *Suzanne Valadon*. New York: Universe Publishing, 1994.

Roskill, Mark, ed. *The Letters of Vincent Van Gogh*. New York: Atheneum, Macmillan Publishing Company, 1963.

Scherer, Deidre, images, and Sandra Haldeman Martz, ed. *Threads of Experience*. Watsonville, CA: Papier-Mache Press, 1996.

Shanks, Ann Zane. *Old Is What You Get: Dialogues on Aging*. New York: The Viking Press, 1976.

Smith, Barbara Lee. *Celebrating the Stitch: Contemporary Embroidery of North America*. Newton, CT: The Taunton Press, 1991.

Starkman, Elaine Marcus. *Learning to Sit in the Silence: A Journal of Caretaking*. Watsonville, CA: Papier-Mache Press, 1993.

Tarkovsky, Andrey. *Sculpting In Time*. Kitty Hunter-Blair, trans. Austin, TX: University of Texas Press, 1986.

Uhde-Stahl, Brigitte. *Paula Modersohn-Becker*. Belser Verlag, trans. Oxford: Phaidon Press Limited, 1990.

FILM

Rafferty, Keven, director. "The Atomic Cafe", 1982.

ORGANIZATIONS

Empowerment for Women in the Arts
Deborah Kruger, founder, workshop and
support group leader
PO Box 1115
Amherst, MA 01004
413-549-4018

Friends of Fiber Art International
P.O.Box 468
Western Springs, IL 60558
708-246-5845

The Graphic Artists Guild
11 West 20th St. 8th Flr.
New York, NY 10011
212-463-7730

The Manitou Project
Pam Mayer
PO Box 117
Williamsville, VT 05362

National Hospice Organization
1901 North Moore Street, Suite 901
Arlington, VA 22209
703-243-5900

Renaissance Press
Paul Taylor
Box 774, 16 Snow Ave.
Hinsdale, NH 03451
603-336-7411

U.S. Friends of the Hanover Infirmary
c/o Dr. Paul Rhodes
1667 Crofton Center, Suite 1
Crofton, MD 21114
410-721-2700

Index of Works

FULLNESS 1992, fabric and thread, 11" x 10", cover of *Learning to Sit in the Silence: A Journal of Caretaking*, (Papier-Mache Press, 1993) Collection of Susan and Lawrence Bailis

Other fine books from C&T

Other titles featuring Deidre Scherer's work, also distributed through C&T Publishing:

For more information write for a free catalog:
C&T Publishing, Inc.
P.O. Box 1456
Lafayette, CA 94549
(800) 284-1114
http://www.ctpub.com
email: ctinfo@ctpub.com